W9-BVO-873

MESOPOTAMIA

ANCIENT CIVILIZATIONS

MESOPOTAMIA

Edited by Sherman Hollar

Britannica
Educational Publishing

IN ASSOCIATION WITH

ROSEN
EDUCATIONAL SERVICES

Published in 2012 by Britannica Educational Publishing
(a trademark of Encyclopædia Britannica, Inc.)
in association with Rosen Educational Services, LLC
29 East 21st Street, New York, NY 10010.

Distributed exclusively by Rosen Educational Services.
For a listing of additional Britannica Educational Publishing titles, call toll free (800) 237-9932.

First Edition

Britannica Educational Publishing
Michael I. Levy: Executive Editor, Encyclopædia Britannica
J.E. Luebering: Director, Core Reference Group, Encyclopædia Britannica
Adam Augustyn: Assistant Manager, Encyclopædia Britannica

Anthony L. Green: Editor, Compton's by Britannica
Michael Anderson: Senior Editor, Compton's by Britannica
Sherman Hollar: Associate Editor, Compton's by Britannica

Marilyn L. Barton: Senior Coordinator, Production Control
Steven Bosco: Director, Editorial Technologies
Lisa S. Braucher: Senior Producer and Data Editor
Yvette Charboneau: Senior Copy Editor
Kathy Nakamura: Manager, Media Acquisition

Rosen Educational Services
Alexandra Hanson-Harding: Editor
Nelson Sá: Art Director
Cindy Reiman: Photography Manager
Matthew Cauli: Designer, Cover Design
Introduction by Alexandra Hanson-Harding

Library of Congress Cataloging-in-Publication Data

Mesopotamia / edited by Sherman Hollar.—1st ed.
    p. cm.—(Ancient civilizations)
"In association with Britannica Educational Publishing, Rosen Educational Services."
Includes bibliographical references and index.
ISBN 978-1-61530-526-1 (library binding)
1. Iraq—Civilization—To 634—Juvenile literature. I. Hollar, Sherman.
DS71.M545 2011
935—dc22

2011007580

Manufactured in the United States of America

On the cover, page 3: An 1852 photo of a winged human-headed bull from the Palace of King Sargon
II, in what is now Khorsabad, Iraq. *Manuel Cohen/Getty Images*

CONTENTS

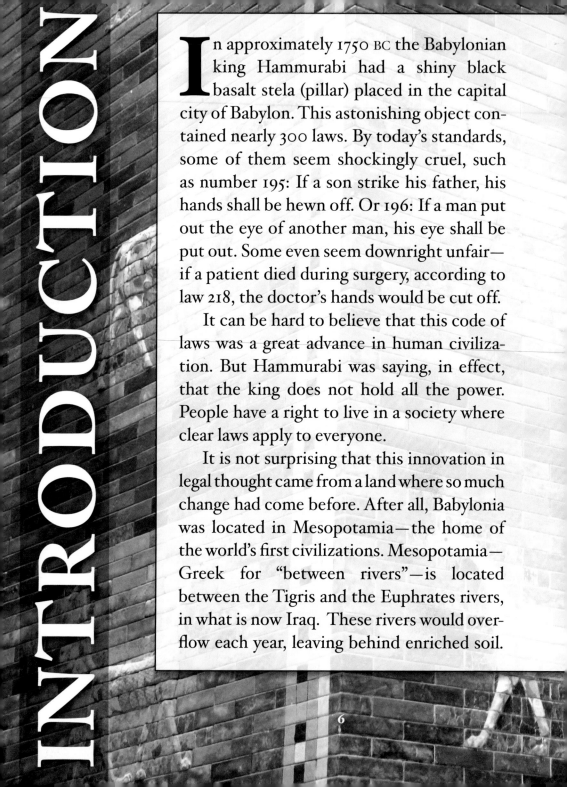

In approximately 1750 BC the Babylonian king Hammurabi had a shiny black basalt stela (pillar) placed in the capital city of Babylon. This astonishing object contained nearly 300 laws. By today's standards, some of them seem shockingly cruel, such as number 195: If a son strike his father, his hands shall be hewn off. Or 196: If a man put out the eye of another man, his eye shall be put out. Some even seem downright unfair—if a patient died during surgery, according to law 218, the doctor's hands would be cut off.

It can be hard to believe that this code of laws was a great advance in human civilization. But Hammurabi was saying, in effect, that the king does not hold all the power. People have a right to live in a society where clear laws apply to everyone.

It is not surprising that this innovation in legal thought came from a land where so much change had come before. After all, Babylonia was located in Mesopotamia—the home of the world's first civilizations. Mesopotamia—Greek for "between rivers"—is located between the Tigris and the Euphrates rivers, in what is now Iraq. These rivers would overflow each year, leaving behind enriched soil.

Starting around 10,000 BC, wandering tribes-people began to grow crops on the fertile land. They gradually stayed in one place, sowing seeds and domesticating animals. Towns, then cities, began to grow.

Mesopotamia is located at the crossroads between Asia, Africa, Europe, and the Arabian Peninsula. That allowed the people

A group of schoolchildren visit the site of Ancient Babylon in 1998. Karim Sahib/AFP/ Getty Images

of this region to trade grain for other goods and get new ideas from other peoples.

A sense of these lively, vivid people comes down to us from their writing. They engraved wedge-shaped letters on small clay tablets in the world's earliest known form of writing, cuneiform. They wrote great stories in cuneiform. They also had a strong sense of private property and would hire scribes to write contracts and keep documents about every object they owned, including items as small as shoes.

In this volume you will learn about four major Mesopotamian civilizations.

The first was Sumer, which began about 3300 BC. The Sumerians contributed to the development of the calendar, metalworking, the wheeled cart, and the potter's wheel. They also created the classic *Epic of Gilgamesh*.

The second great empire you'll learn about is Babylonia. The Babylonians added to the knowledge of astronomy, mathematics, and law. Their greatest king, Hammurabi, came to rule in about 1792 BC. Aside from his laws, Hammurabi is credited with expanding his empire.

In about 1400 BC the Assyrians of the north freed themselves from Babylon's control. Fierce and warlike, they were the first to use horses as cavalry. They built roads and organized a mail service for communication. Despite their ferocity, their art and architecture were magnificent. The Assyrian king Sargon II built a 1,000-room palace near Assyria's capital, Nineveh. Huge human-headed winged bulls and lions, carved in alabaster, guarded the gates of Assyrian palaces and temples. The Assyrians also preserved cuneiform texts in great libraries.

Next, the Chaldeans took over and rebuilt Babylon into a rich and gorgeous city starting around 606 BC. An example of the city's beauties was the Hanging Gardens of Babylon, an ancient wonder of the world. The Chaldeans also made progress in astronomy and math. But in 539 BC, they became a part of the Persian Empire.

The people of ancient Mesopotamia made vital contributions to a broad range of fields, including government, law, literature, architecture, and astronomy, among many others. Perhaps Hammurabi's rule seems harsh, but the idea of sharing a code of laws is deeply ingrained today in every civilized society. For that, we owe a debt to the people of Mesopotamia.

CHAPTER 1

MESOPOTAMIA— THE BIRTHPLACE OF CIVILIZATION

The area between the Tigris and Euphrates rivers in what is now Iraq is the site of ancient Mesopotamia, birthplace of the world's first civilizations. The name is Greek for "land between the rivers." As the muddy streams flooded and receded, their silt built a plain with rich soil, ideal for agriculture. Tradition locates the biblical Garden of Eden in Mesopotamia.

The nomadic peoples of the Arabian Desert on the west and what are now Iran and Turkey on the east and north coveted the fertile river basin. From the earliest times successive tribes swept into it and fought to possess it, founding their nations and then falling in turn before more powerful foes.

Since 1840 groups of archaeologists have excavated sites in Mesopotamia and have found signs that there were primitive settlements here as far back as 10,000 BC. In about 3300 BC the Sumerians, a non-Semitic people from the east, abandoned their wandering tent-dwelling existence and settled in

As Mesopotamian people have been doing for thousands of years, an Iraqi man collects the wheat harvest. This field is near the marshes crossing the southern Iraqi town of al-Azeir. **Essam Al-Sudani/AFP/ Getty Images**

an area called the Plain of Shinar. Here they tilled the soil, built houses, and constructed irrigation systems, draining marshes and digging canals, dikes, and ditches. The need for cooperation on these large irrigation projects led to the growth of government and law. The Sumerians are thus credited with forming the earliest of the major ancient civilizations of this region.

This model represents an early brick dwelling from the ancient Mesopotamian settlement of Jericho, around 5000 BC. The walls are of packed mud blocks, made of fine clay mixed with straw. **SSPL via Getty Images**

GEOGRAPHY OF MESOPOTAMIA

The flat Mesopotamian plain is very fertile. The land was built up of mud and clay deposited by two great rivers, the Tigris and the Euphrates. These twin rivers come down from mountains in the north, cut southeastward through hilly grasslands, and finally cross the plain they created to reach the Persian Gulf.

TIGRIS RIVER

The streams that join to form the Tigris River begin in high mountains that rim Lake

This map shows the course of the Tigris and Euphrates rivers.

Van in eastern Turkey. Leaving Turkey, the Tigris touches the northeastern border of Syria and then flows southeastward across Iraq. In Iraq it is joined by tributaries from the east—principally the Great Zab, Little Zab, and Diyala. The Euphrates, west of the Tigris, runs in the same general direction.

In ancient times the two rivers had separate mouths. Now they meet in a swamp in southern Iraq and form a single stream, the Shatt al 'Arab, which flows into the head of the Persian Gulf. The Tigris, 1,180 miles (1,900 kilometers) long, is shorter than the Euphrates, but it is more important commercially because its channel is deeper.

The Tigris was the great river of the kingdom of Assyria. The ancient city of Assur, which gave its name to Assyria, stood on its banks, as did Nineveh, Assyria's splendid capital. Much later the Macedonian general Seleucus built his capital city Seleucia on the Tigris, and across the river from Seleucia the Parthian kings built Ctesiphon. The chief cities on the river today are Baghdad, the capital of Iraq, and Mosul, farther upstream. Basra, on the Shatt al 'Arab, is Iraq's major port.

Since ancient times the people of Mesopotamia have depended on the water of the two rivers to irrigate their hot, dry land. The soil itself is largely a gift of the rivers, which deposit tremendous quantities of silt on their lower course and in the northern part of the Persian Gulf. As a result of these deposits, ruins of cities that were once gulf ports now lie far inland.

EUPHRATES RIVER

The longest river of western Asia is the 1,700-mile (2,700-kilometer) Euphrates. It begins in the high mountains of eastern Turkey, crosses eastern Syria, and then flows southeastward through the length of Iraq. Because of Iraq's hot, dry climate much of the river's water is lost through evaporation and use for irrigation. The river receives most of its water from winter rains and snowfall. It is navigable only by flat-bottomed riverboats.

The Tigris runs almost parallel with the Euphrates and together they form a great, agriculturally productive alluvial plain—that is, a plain made of silt, sand, clay, and gravel that is deposited by rivers. There are two flood periods each year. The major tributaries of the Euphrates are the Balikh, Al Khabur, and Gharraf Channel.

Fishermen return from work on a flat boat in the Euphrates River in southern Iraq in 2003. Ahmad Al-Rubaye/AFP/Getty Images

PEOPLES OF THE REGION

Three main peoples contributed to the civilization of Mesopotamia. The earliest were the Sumerians. They lived in a small county-sized area located around the mouths of the two rivers in a land called Sumer (in the Bible, Shinar). These non-Semitic people, who probably came from Anatolia (Asia Minor) in about 3300 BC, developed a culture that spread to nearby Semitic peoples. By 1800 BC political power had moved north up the Euphrates to the Semitic city of Babylon in Akkad. The entire plain then became known as Babylonia. Centuries later the center of power moved north once more to warlike Assyria, in the rolling hill country of the upper Tigris Valley.

Before the Sumerians appeared on the land, it had been occupied by a non-Semitic people, referred to as Ubaidians. Their name comes from the village of Al Ubaid, in which their remains were first found by archaeologists.

The Ubaidians settled the region between 4500 and 4000 BC. They drained the marshes and introduced agriculture. They also developed trade based on small handicraft industries such as metalwork, leather goods, and pottery.

Excavations have uncovered Ubaidian remains throughout southern Mesopotamia. The hallmark of the period was a painted pottery decorated with geometric and sometimes floral and animal designs in dark paint on a buff or drab clay. Many vessels seem to have been made on a slow wheel, and they had loop handles and spouts (the first historical occurrence of these).

THE WORLD'S FIRST CITIES

In ancient Mesopotamia, a land of blazing sun and very little rainfall, irrigation was vital for farming. Centuries before the beginning of known history, the Sumerians undertook the stupendous task of building embankments to control the floodwaters of the Euphrates River. Gradually they drained the marshes and dug irrigation canals and ditches. Large-scale cooperation was needed to build the irrigation works, keep them in repair, and apportion the water.

Ancient frieze of a Mesopotamian man holding a piece of pottery. **Ahmad Al-Rubaye/AFP/ Getty Images**

The rich soil produced abundant crops of barley, emmer (a kind of wheat), beans, olives, grapes, and flax.

For the first time there was a surplus to feed city workers such as artists, craftsmen, and merchants. This great change in living habits brought about civilization—defined as a city-based society held together by economic enterprises. There were no nations then, only small city-states. At a time when only the most rudimentary forms of transportation and communication were available, the city-state was the most governable type of human settlement. City-states were ruled by leaders, called *ensis*, who were probably authorized to control the local irrigation systems.

The Sumerians built their villages on artificial mounds to protect them from floods. Very early they learned to make bricks in molds and dry them in the sun or bake them in kilns. Their sturdy houses were small and crowded close together on narrow lanes. Some were two or more stories high. The whole city was surrounded by a wall for protection. Outside the wall were the poor people's huts, built of reeds that were plastered with clay.

Each Sumerian city rose up around the shrine of a local god. As a reflection of a

Whole emmer wheat. **Armstrong Studios/FoodPix/Getty Images**

city's wealth, its temple became an elaborate structure. The temple buildings stood on a spacious raised platform reached by staircases and ramps. From the platform rose the temple tower, called a ziggurat (holy mountain), with a circular staircase or ramp around the outside. On the temple grounds were quarters for priests, officials, accountants, musicians, and singers; treasure chambers; storehouses for grain, tools, and weapons; and workshops for bakers, pottery makers, brewers, leatherworkers, spinners and weavers, and jewelers.

There were also pens for keeping the sheep and goats that were destined for sacrifice to the temple god.

Horses and camels were still unknown, but sheep, goats, oxen, donkeys, and dogs had been domesticated. The plow had been invented, and the wheel, made from a solid piece of wood, was used for carts and for shaping pottery. Oxen pulled the carts and plows; donkeys served as pack animals. Bulky goods were moved by boat on the rivers and canals. The boats were usually hauled from

An Iraqi woman, wearing traditional clothes and jewelry, plays a Sumerian musical instrument during an exhibition at the ministry of culture in Baghdad in 2006. **Sabah Arar/AFP/Getty Images**

the banks, but sails also were in use. Before 3000 BC the Sumerians had learned to make tools and weapons by smelting copper with tin to make bronze, a much harder metal than copper alone.

Mud, clay, and reeds were the only materials the Sumerians had in abundance. Trade was therefore necessary to supply the city workers with materials. Merchants went out

One of the oldest known bronze relief bowls from ancient Mesopotamia is displayed here. **Behrouz Mehri/AFP/Getty Images**

in overland caravans or in ships to exchange the products of Sumerian industry for wood, stone, and metals. There are indications that Sumerian sailing vessels even reached the valley of the Indus River in India. The chief route, however, was around the Fertile Crescent, between the Arabian Desert and the northern mountains. This route led up the valley of the two rivers, westward to Syria, and down the Mediterranean coast.

MESOPOTAMIAN CLOTHING

From statues and other evidence, it is clear that the people of Mesopotamia were very concerned about fashion. In the early years of the Sumerian civilization, both sexes wore sheepskin skirts with the skin turned inside and the wool combed into decorative tufts. These wraparound skirts were pinned in place and extended from the waist to the knees or, for more important persons, to the ankles. The upper part of the torso was bare or clothed by another sheepskin cloaking the shoulders. From about 2500 BC a woven woolen fabric replaced the sheepskin, but the tufted effect was retained, either by sewing tufts onto the garment or by weaving loops into the fabric. At this time, also, long

cloaks were worn, and materials included felted wool and leather.

Both sexes seem to have often worn large wigs. They also both wore elaborate golden jewelry encrusted with semiprecious stones, including brooches, earrings, hair ornaments, and neck chains. A different style of dress is evident in Mesopotamian sculptures dating after about 2370 BC. Both men and women were clothed in a large piece of wool or linen draped around the body over a skirt. This garment, similar to a shawl, was characteristically edged with fringe. For men, the fabric was arranged so that the fullness was at the rear, leaving the sword arm free.

The dress worn in Mesopotamia by the Babylonians (2105–1240 BC) and the Assyrians (1200–540 BC) included two basic garments for both sexes: the tunic and the shawl, each cut from one piece of material. The knee- or ankle-length tunic had short sleeves and a round neckline. Over it were draped one or more shawls held in position by a broad belt. Decoration was rich, in chiefly geometric

This frieze from the Iraq Museum shows fashionable Mesopotamian men with well-tended beards and elegant clothes. **AFP/Getty Images**

allover patterns or in borders. Women wore a short skirt as underwear, men a loincloth. Sandals or boots for both sexes was made from fabric or soft leather.

Both men and women grew their hair long. It was carefully curled and ringleted, with false hair added if needed. Perfumes, oils, and black dye were used on the hair. Men grew long, carefully tended curled beards. A band of metal or fabric encircled the brow, or a woolen, felt, or leather cap was worn.

AKKAD

Akkad was an ancient region in what is now central Iraq. Akkad was the northern (or northwestern) division of ancient Babylonian civilization. The region was located roughly in the area where the Tigris and Euphrates rivers are closest to each other, and its northern limit extended beyond the line of the modern cities of Al-Fallujah and Baghdad. The early inhabitants of this region were predominantly Semitic, and their speech is called

An ancient Iraqi bronze statuette depicting a standing woman in a position of prayer on display in the Egyptian Museum in Cairo in 2009. **AFP/ Getty Images**

Akkadian. To the south of the region of Akkad lay Sumer.

The name of Akkad was taken from the city of Agade, which was founded by the Semitic conqueror Sargon in about 2300 BC. Sargon united the various city-states in the region and extended his rule to encompass much of Mesopotamia. After the fall of Sargon's dynasty in about 2150 BC, the central Iraq region was ruled by a state jointly composed of Sumerians and Akkadians.

Under the kings of Akkad, Akkadian became a literary language that was written with the cuneiform system of writing. Akkadian is the oldest Semitic dialect still preserved.

CHAPTER 2
SUMERIAN CIVILIZATION

Among many other achievements, the Sumerians contributed to the development of metalworking, wheeled carts, and potter's wheels. They may have invented the first form of writing. They engraved pictures on clay tablets in a form of writing known as cuneiform. The tablets were used to keep the accounts of the temple food storehouses. By about 2500 BC these picture-signs were being refined into an alphabet.

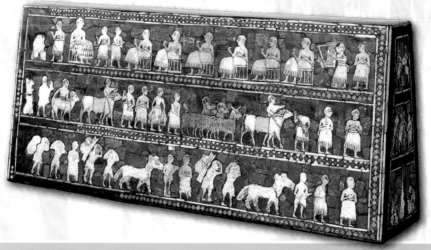

A richly decorated object called the Stanard of Ur was found in the royal cemetery at Ur, an important city in southern Mesopotamia. It dates to about 2500 BC. Its two main panels depict scenes of peace (shown) and war in mosaic inlays of lapis lazuli, shell, colored stone, and mother-of-pearl. **Courtesy of the trustees of the British Museum**

The Sumerians developed the first calendar, which they adjusted to the phases of the Moon. The lunar calendar was adopted by the Semites, Egyptians, and Greeks. An increase in trade between Sumerian cities and between Sumeria and other, more distant regions led to the growth of a merchant class.

THE SUMERIAN WRITING SYSTEM

Whether the Sumerians were the first to develop writing is uncertain, but theirs is the oldest known writing system. The clay tablets on which they wrote were very durable when baked. Archaeologists have dug up many thousands of them—some dated earlier than 3000 BC.

The earliest writing of the Sumerians was picture writing similar in some ways to Egyptian hieroglyphs. They began to develop their special style when they found that on soft, wet clay it was easier to impress a line than to scratch it. To draw the pictures they used a stylus—probably a straight piece of reed with a three-cornered end.

An unexpected result came about: the stylus could best produce triangular forms (wedges) and straight lines. Curved lines

The First Calendar

People have kept track of the days by the march of daylight and darkness and of the changing seasons in order to know when to plant crops and to get ready for winter. Sometimes they kept the record by notching a stick or knotting a cord once every day. They also watched the changing positions of the Sun and stars, the changes of the Moon, and the habits of plants and animals. The making of an exact calendar, however, has perplexed humankind for ages because the natural divisions of time by days (Earth cycle), months (lunar cycle), and years (solar cycle) do not fit together perfectly.

The Sumerians were the first people to make a calendar. They used the phases of the Moon, counting 12 lunar months as a year. To make up for the difference between this year and the solar year of the seasons, they inserted an extra month in the calendar about every four years. The early Egyptians, Greeks, and Semitic peoples copied this calendar.

The seven-day week, which has no astronomical basis, was also apparently first observed in Mesopotamia. It was introduced to Rome in the 1st century AD by Persian astrologers who associated each day with a different planet; when Christianity became the official religion of Rome in the 4th century, the seven-day week was adopted by the state and spread throughout the Roman Empire.

therefore had to be broken up into a series of straight strokes. Pictures lost their form and became stylized symbols. This kind of writing on clay is called cuneiform, from the Latin *cuneus*, meaning "wedge."

A tremendous step forward was accomplished when the symbols came to be associated with the sound of the thing shown rather than with the idea of the thing itself. Each sign then represented a syllable. Although cuneiform writing was still used long after the alphabet appeared, it never fully developed an alphabet.

SUMERIAN SCHOOLS

Cuneiform was difficult to learn. To master it children usually went to a temple school. Using a clay tablet as a textbook, the teacher wrote on the left-hand side, and the pupil copied the model on the right. Any mistakes could be smoothed out. The pupil began by making single wedges in various positions and then went on to groups of wedges. Thousands of groups had to be mastered.

Stylus found in 1924 at the ancient Sumerian city of Kish, revealing the method used in making cuneiform signs. **Mansell/Time & Life Pictures/ Getty Images**

CUNEIFORM

The most widely used and historically significant writing system of the ancient Middle East was called cuneiform. The writing system was in use at least by the end of the 4th millennium BC, and during the 3rd millennium the pictures that it used became fairly standardized linear drawings.

Cuneiform was not a language. It was, like Egyptian hieroglyphics and the Chinese system of ideographs, or ideograms, a picture-writing system that used symbols. As the symbols gained acceptance throughout the Middle East, they could be understood by all ethnic groups even though the groups spoke different languages and dialects.

The earliest known documents in cuneiform were written by the Sumerians of southern Mesopotamia, who assigned their own word-sounds to the symbols. Later, the Akkadians adopted the symbols but pronounced them as corresponding Akkadian words. Cuneiform thus passed successively from one people to another. The Akkadians were succeeded by the Babylonians, and they by the Assyrians.

The expansion of cuneiform writing outside Mesopotamia began during the 3rd millennium BC, when the country of Elam, in what is now southwestern Iran, adopted the system. The Hurrians of northern Mesopotamia adopted Akkadian cuneiform

The Flood Tablet, 11th cuneiform tablet in a series relating the Gilgamesh epic, from Nineveh, 7th century BC; in the British Museum, London. © Photos.com/Jupiterimages

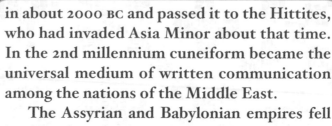

in about 2000 BC and passed it to the Hittites, who had invaded Asia Minor about that time. In the 2nd millennium cuneiform became the universal medium of written communication among the nations of the Middle East.

The Assyrian and Babylonian empires fell in the 7th and 6th centuries BC. By this time Aramaic was becoming the common language of the area, and Phoenician script came into general use. Cuneiform was used less and less, though many priests and scholars kept the writing form alive until the 1st century AD. Cuneiform owes its disappearance largely to the fact that it was a nonalphabetic way of writing. It could not compete successfully with the alphabetic systems being developed by the Phoenicians, Israelites, Greeks, and other peoples of the Mediterranean.

Finally the pupil was assigned a book to copy, but the work was slow and laborious. Many first chapters of all the important Sumerian works have been handed down from students' tablets, but only fragments of the rest of the books survive.

A statue of a scribe from the Sumerian era, in the collection of the Iraq Museum in Baghdad. **AFP/Getty Images**

The pupils also studied arithmetic. The Sumerians based their number system on 10, but they multiplied 10 by 6 to get the next unit. They multiplied 60 by 10, then multiplied 600 by 6, and so on. (The number 60 has the advantage of being divisible by 2, 3, 4, 5, 6, 10, 12, 15, 20, and 30.) The Sumerians also divided the circle into 360 degrees. From these early people came the word *dozen* (a fifth of 60) and the division of the clock to measure hours, minutes, and seconds.

The Sumerians had standard measures, with units of length, area, and capacity. Their standard weight was the mina, made up of 60 shekels—about the same weight as a pound. There was no coined money. Standard weights of silver served as measures of value and as a means of exchange.

From the earliest times the Sumerians had a strong sense of private property. After they learned to write and figure, they kept documents about every acquired object, including such small items as shoes. Every business transaction had to be recorded. Near the gates of the cities, scribes would sit ready to sell their services. Their hands would move fast over a lump of clay, turning the stylus. Then the contracting parties added their signatures by means of seals. The usual seal was an engraved cylinder of stone or metal that could be rolled over wet clay.

In the course of time cuneiform was used for every purpose, just as writing is today—for letters, narratives, prayers and incantations, dictionaries, even mathematical and astronomical treatises. The Babylonians and Assyrians adapted cuneiform for their own

In the Iraq Museum in Baghdad, four cylinder seals with representations of Gilgamesh and Enkidu from approximately 2500 BC. **Roger Viollet/Getty Images**

Semitic languages and spread its use to neighboring Syria, Anatolia, Armenia, and Iran.

STORIES OF GODS AND HEROES

As the people in a city-state became familiar with the gods of other cities, they worked out relationships between them, just as the Greeks and Romans did in their myths centuries later. Sometimes two or more gods came to be viewed as one. Eventually a ranking order developed among the gods. Anu, a sky god who originally had been the city god of Uruk, came to be regarded as the greatest of them all—the god of the heavens. His closest rival was the storm god of the air, Enlil of Nippur. The great gods were worshiped in the temples. Each family had little clay figures of its own household gods and small houses or wall niches for them.

The Sumerians believed that their ancestors had created the ground they lived on by separating it from the water. According to their creation myth, the world was once watery chaos. The mother of Chaos was Tiamat, an immense dragon. When the gods appeared to bring order out of Chaos, Tiamat created an army of dragons. Enlil called the winds to his aid. Tiamat came forward, her mouth wide open. Enlil pushed the winds inside her and she swelled up so that she could not move. Then Enlil split her body open. He laid half of the body flat to form the Earth, with the other half arched over it to form the sky. The gods then beheaded Tiamat's husband and created mankind from his blood, mixed with clay.

The longest story is the Gilgamesh epic, one of the outstanding works of ancient literature. The superhero Gilgamesh originally appeared in Sumerian mythology as a legendary king of Uruk. A long Babylonian poem includes an account of his journey to the bottom of the sea to obtain the plant of life.

Another searcher for eternal life was Adapa, a fisherman who gained wisdom from Ea, the god of water. The other gods were jealous of his knowledge and called him to heaven. Ea warned him not to drink or eat while there. Anu offered him the water of life and the bread of life because he thought that, since Adapa already knew too much, he might as well be a god. Adapa, however, refused and went back to Earth to die, thus losing for himself and for mankind the gift of immortal life. These legends somewhat resemble the Bible story of Adam and Eve. It is highly probable, in fact, that the ancient legends and myths

of Mesopotamia supplied material that was reworked by the biblical authors.

It was during the Sumerian era that a great flood overwhelmed Mesopotamia. So great was this flood that stories about it worked their way into several ancient literatures. The Sumerian counterpart of Noah was Ziusudra, and from him was developed the Babylonian figure Utnapishtim, whose story of the flood was related in the *Epic of Gilgamesh*. Immortal after his escape from the flood, Utnapishtim was also the wise man who told Gilgamesh where to find a youth-restoring plant.

THE LAST OF THE SUMERIANS

Within a few centuries the Sumerians had built up a society based in 12 city-states: Kish, Uruk (in the Bible, Erech), Ur, Sippar, Akshak, Larak, Nippur, Adab, Umma, Lagash, Bad-tibira, and Larsa. According to one of the earliest historical documents, the Sumerian King List, eight kings of Sumer reigned before the famous flood. Afterwards various city-states by turns became the temporary seat of power until about 2800 BC, when they were united under the rule of one king—Etana of Kish.

Gilgamesh

The fullest extant text of the Gilgamesh epic is on 12 incomplete Akkadian-language tablets found at Nineveh in the library of the Assyrian king Ashurbanipal. The gaps that occur in the tablets have been partly filled by various fragments found elsewhere in Mesopotamia and Anatolia. In addition, five short poems in the Sumerian language are known; the poems have been titled "Gilgamesh and Huwawa," "Gilgamesh and the Bull of Heaven," "Gilgamesh and Agga of Kish," "Gilgamesh, Enkidu, and the Netherworld," and "The Death of Gilgamesh."

The Ninevite version of the epic begins with a prologue in praise of Gilgamesh, part divine and part human, the great builder and warrior, knower of all things on land and sea. In order to curb Gilgamesh's seemingly harsh rule, the god Anu caused the creation of Enkidu, a wild man who at first lived among animals. Soon, however, Enkidu was initiated into the ways of city life and traveled to Uruk, where Gilgamesh awaited him. Tablet II describes a trial of strength between the two men in which Gilgamesh was the victor; thereafter, Enkidu was the friend and companion (in Sumerian texts, the servant) of Gilgamesh. In Tablets III–V the two men set out together against Huwawa (Humbaba), the divinely appointed guardian of a remote

Gilgamesh is the best known of all ancient Mesopotamian heroes. Numerous tales in the Akkadian language have been told about Gilgamesh, and the whole collection has been described as an odyssey—the odyssey of a king who did not want to die. Stock Montage/Archive Photos/Getty Images

cedar forest, but the rest of the engagement is not recorded in the surviving fragments. In Tablet VI Gilgamesh, who had returned to Uruk, rejected the marriage proposal of Ishtar, the goddess of love, and then, with Enkidu's aid, killed the divine bull that she had sent to destroy him. Tablet VII begins with Enkidu's account of a dream in which the gods Anu, Ea, and Shamash decided that he must die for slaying the bull. Enkidu then fell ill and dreamed of the "house of dust" that awaited him. Gilgamesh's lament for his friend and the state funeral of Enkidu are narrated in Tablet VIII. Afterward, Gilgamesh made a dangerous journey (Tablets IX and X) in search of Utnapishtim, the survivor of the Babylonian flood, in order to learn from him how to escape death. He finally reached Utnapishtim, who told him the story of the flood and showed him where to find a plant that would renew youth (Tablet XI). But after Gilgamesh obtained the plant, it was seized by a serpent, and Gilgamesh unhappily returned to Uruk. An appendage to the epic, Tablet XII, related the loss of objects called *pukku* and *mikku* (perhaps "drum" and "drumstick") given to Gilgamesh by Ishtar. The epic ends with the return of the spirit of Enkidu, who promised to recover the objects and then gave a grim report on the underworld.

Ancient Ur

Advisor   King of Ur

After Etana, the city-states vied for domination; this weakened the Sumerians, and they were ripe for conquest—first by Elamites, then by Akkadians.

The Sumerians had never been very warlike, and they had only a citizen army, called to arms in time of danger. In about 2340 BC King Sargon of Akkad conquered them and went on to build an empire that stretched westward to the Mediterranean Sea. The empire, though short-lived, fostered art and literature.

Led by Ur, the Sumerians again spread their rule far westward. During Ur's supremacy (about 2150 to 2050 BC) Sumerian culture reached its highest development. Shortly thereafter the cities lost their independence forever, and gradually the Sumerians completely disappeared as a people. Their language, however, lived on as the language of culture. Their writing, their business organization, their scientific knowledge, and their mythology and law were spread westward by the Babylonians and Assyrians.

Illustration of an advisor and the King of Ur. **Buyenlarge/Archive Photos/Getty Images**

The Sumerians were conquered by their Semitic neighbors. But their civilization was carried on by their successors—the Akkadians, Babylonians, Assyrians, and Chaldeans.

Like the Sumerians, the Babylonians made distinct contributions to the growth of civilization. They added to the knowledge of astronomy, advanced the knowledge of mathematics, and built the first great capital city, Babylon. The

Dark stone pillar bearing inscribed laws of Hammurabi and an illustration of the king before the sun god Shamash at the Louvre Museum in Paris. **Time & Life Pictures/Getty Images**

Babylonian King Hammurabi set forth the Code of Hammurabi, the most complete compilation of Babylonian law and one of the first great law codes in the world.

THE REIGN OF HAMMURABI

During the first thousand years of its known history, Babylon was a mere village. It became the capital of the kingdom of Babylon in about 1894 BC. The kingdom's brilliant First Dynasty lasted 300 years and reached its greatest glory under King Hammurabi. He spread the rule of Babylon south into Sumer and west around the Fertile Crescent into Syria. He was most famous, however, for the code he published to unify the legal practices in his empire.

The dates of Hammurabi's life and reign are uncertain. It is believed that he succeeded his father, Sinmuballit, in 1792 BC. Knowledge of the events of his life is derived from historical and building inscriptions, the prologue to his laws, his correspondence, and other materials. The length of his reign is established by what are called date formulas—the naming of years for significant accomplishments or acts of the king.

Hammurabi is credited with uniting most of the area between the Tigris and the

The archaeological site of Uruk on January 25, 2010. Uruk was renowned for its walls, which were first built 4,700 years ago. **Essam Al-Sudani/AFP/Getty Images**

Euphrates under one extensive empire for the first time since Sargon of Akkad did so in about 2300 BC. To do this, Hammurabi waged several military campaigns. The purpose of most of his operations was to gain control of the Tigris and Euphrates waters, on which agricultural productivity depended. Some campaigns were over control of trade routes or access to mines in Iran.

The king began his military campaigns in 1787 by conquering the cities of Uruk and Isin to the south. He then turned his attention to the northwest and east. The power of Assyria prevented him from achieving any significant results, and for 20 years no major warlike activity was reported. He used the time to fortify cities on his northern borders.

The last 14 years of Hammurabi's reign were overshadowed by war. In 1763 he fought against a coalition east of the Tigris that threatened to block access to metal-producing areas in Iran. The same year he conquered the city of Larsa, which enabled him to take over the older Sumerian cities in the south. He followed this victory with the conquest of Mari, 250 miles (400 kilometers) upstream on the Euphrates. During his last two years the king concentrated on building defense fortifications. By this time he was a sick man, and the government was in the hands of his son, Samsuiluna.

Hammurabi effected great changes in all spheres of life. Most of his rule was given to the establishment of law and order, religious buildings, irrigation projects, and defense works. He personally oversaw the administration of government. In doing so he failed to create a permanent bureaucratic system.

HAMMURABI'S CODE OF LAWS

The Code of Hammurabi is the most complete remnant of Babylonian law. The background to the code is the body of Sumerian law under which city-states had lived for centuries. The code itself was advanced far beyond ancient tribal customs. The stela (a usually carved or inscribed stone slab or pillar used for commemorative purposes) on which the code is inscribed originally stood in Babylon's temple of Marduk, the national god. It was discovered at the site of ancient Susa in 1901 by the French archaeologist Jean-Vincent Scheil. He presented it to the Louvre.

The code consists of 282 case laws, or judicial decisions, collected toward the end of Hammurabi's reign. The decisions deal with such matters as family, marriage, and divorce; tariffs; trade and commerce; prices; and criminal and civil law. From the code it is evident that there were distinct social classes, each of which had its rights and obligations. The right of private property was recognized, though most of the land was in the hands of the royal house. Ownership of land brought with it the duty to provide men for the army and public works.

Families were dominated by fathers. Marriages were arranged by parents, and

A view of part of the Code of Hammurabi. Kean
Collection/Archive Photos/Getty Images

control of the children by the father was unlimited until marriage. Adoption was common, either to ensure continuance of a family line or to perpetuate a business.

In criminal law the ruling principle for punishment was the ancient *lex talionis*, or law of retaliation. Penalties were calculated according to the nature of the offense. Capital punishment was common, and the various means of execution were prescribed, depending on the nature of the crime. Neither imprisonment nor forced labor is mentioned in the code. Unintended manslaughter was punished by a fine. Willful murder was not mentioned. Carelessness and neglect in the performance of work was severely punished. In general, the penalties prescribed were an improvement over the brutality of previous law.

This failure was a primary reason for the rapid deterioration of his empire after his death. Hammurabi's accomplishments are believed by historians to be exaggerated. This is partly because of the fame he gained when his law code was discovered. His lasting achievement was to shift the main theater of Mesopotamian history northward, where it remained for 1,000 years.

BABYLONIAN LANGUAGE AND RELIGION

Hammurabi made his own Semitic language official throughout his kingdom and raised the god of Babylon, Marduk, to first place among the deities. Scholars rewrote old Sumerian myths and gave Marduk, rather than Enlil, credit for creating the universe. The Babylonians' chief female deity was the ancient mother goddess Innini of Uruk, renamed Ishtar.

The goddess Ishtar in ivory, 900-800 BC. **Time & Life Pictures/Getty Images**

THE ZIGGURATS OF MESOPOTAMIA

The pyramidal, stepped temple towers known as ziggurats were characteristic of the major cities of Mesopotamia from approximately 2200 until 500 BC. A ziggurat was always built with a core of mud brick and an exterior covered with baked brick. It had no internal chambers and was usually square or rectangular, averaging either 170 feet (50 meters) square or 125 × 170 feet (40 × 50 meters) at the base. Approximately 25 ziggurats are known, being equally divided among Sumer, Babylonia, and Assyria.

No ziggurat is preserved to its original height. Ascent was by an exterior triple stairway or by a spiral ramp, but for almost half of the known ziggurats, no means of ascent has been discovered. The sloping sides and terraces were often landscaped with trees and shrubs. The best-preserved ziggurat is at Ur (modern Tall al-Muqayyar, Iraq). The largest, at Choghā Zanbīl in Elam (now in southwestern Iran), is 335 feet (102 meters) square and 80 feet (24 meters) high and stands at less than half its estimated original height. A ziggurat, apparently of great antiquity, is located at Tepe Sialk in modern Kāshān, Iran. The legendary Tower of Babel has been popularly associated with the ziggurat of the great temple of Marduk in Babylon.

Ziggurat at Choghā Zanbīl near Susa, Iran. Robert Harding Picture Library/ Sybil Sassoon

As goddess of fertility, Ishtar could grant her worshipers crops, lambs, or children. In the hot midsummer month named for her son Tammuz, vegetation dried up and people fasted until he rose from the dead to make the earth green again. The worship of Ishtar (also called Astarte) and Tammuz spread over southwestern Asia and reached Egypt in the myth of Isis and Osiris. Later the deities appeared in Greece as Demeter and Persephone.

CHAPTER 4
THE ASSYRIANS AND THE CHALDEANS

Formerly a dependency of Babylonia, Assyria emerged as an independent state in the 14th century BC, and in the subsequent period it became a major power in Mesopotamia. Famous for their cruelty and fighting prowess, the Assyrians were also monumental builders, as shown by archaeological sites at Nineveh, Assur, and Nimrud. From the mid-8th to the late 7th century BC, a series of strong Assyrian kings united most of the Middle East, from Egypt to the Persian Gulf, under Assyrian rule. The last great Assyrian ruler was Ashurbanipal, who died in 626 BC.

When Assyria declined, Babylon rose once more to wealth and imperial power under the great Chaldean king Nebuchadnezzar II. This king is remembered in the Old Testament for his destruction of Jerusalem and the Babylonian captivity of the Jewish people. In Babylonia, however, he was celebrated as the builder who made Babylon the most splendid city in the world.

Ashurbanipal, king of Assyria. **Hulton Archive/Getty Images**

THE KINGDOM OF ASSYRIA

After Hammurabi's death, wave after wave of Indo-European tribes invaded from the northern mountains. For centuries the entire civilized world was plunged into darkness.

The Hyksos invaded Egypt. The Kassites overran Babylonia. The Hurrians occupied the rest of the Fertile Crescent, from Assyria into Palestine. This period has been called the Middle Ages of antiquity. In about 1400 BC the Assyrians freed themselves from the invaders' rule. Then they extended their kingdom northward.

Assyria took its name from its chief city, Assur, on the upper Tigris. Lying north of Babylonia, on the great trade route of the Fertile Crescent, the country was frequently invaded from the north as well as from the south. Constant warfare made the Assyrians fierce fighters, and traders who passed their way were forced to pay them tribute for protection.

The Assyrians had long been under the control of Babylon and had absorbed Babylonian culture. Like the Babylonians they were Semites, and their language was almost identical with the Babylonians'. From the Hittites of Anatolia they learned the use of iron and developed powerful weapons to build up a military state. From them they also acquired horses and were the first to use them in war as cavalry instead of for drawing chariots. In order to strike terror into the hearts of their enemies, they boasted of their cruelties.

The citadel of Khorsabad in Assyria, as it may have appeared in the time of Sargon II (722–705 BC), is illustrated in a reconstruction drawing by Charles Altman. **Courtesy of the Oriental Institute, the University of Chicago**

Assyria's greatest period of expansion took place as the power of the Hittites and Egyptians over Syria and Palestine gradually weakened. The Assyrian king Tiglath-Pileser III (745–727 BC) took Damascus, in Syria. Sargon II (722–705 BC), most famous of Assyrian kings, made Israel an Assyrian province and carried into the interior of his empire 30,000 Israelites (the so-called Ten Lost Tribes of Israel). His son Sennacherib (705–681 BC) conquered Sidon, in Phoenicia, but Tyre resisted his assault. Esarhaddon (681–668 BC) conquered Egypt. Ashurbanipal (668–626 BC), the last of the great Assyrian kings, subdued Elam, east of Mesopotamia, and extended the empire to its greatest size. Roads were built to enable the Assyrian armies to subdue rebels quickly. A highly organized mail service carried messages from the court to faraway governors.

North of Nineveh, Sargon II built a palace far surpassing anything seen before his day. It covered 25 acres (10 hectares) and had nearly 1,000 rooms. Near it stood a seven-story ziggurat temple. Sennacherib put up three magnificent palaces in his capital at Nineveh. The Babylonians had covered their brick walls with glazed brickwork of many colors, but the Assyrians faced theirs with delicately carved slabs of limestone or glowing alabaster. Colossal human-headed winged bulls or lions, carved in alabaster, stood guard outside the main gates of

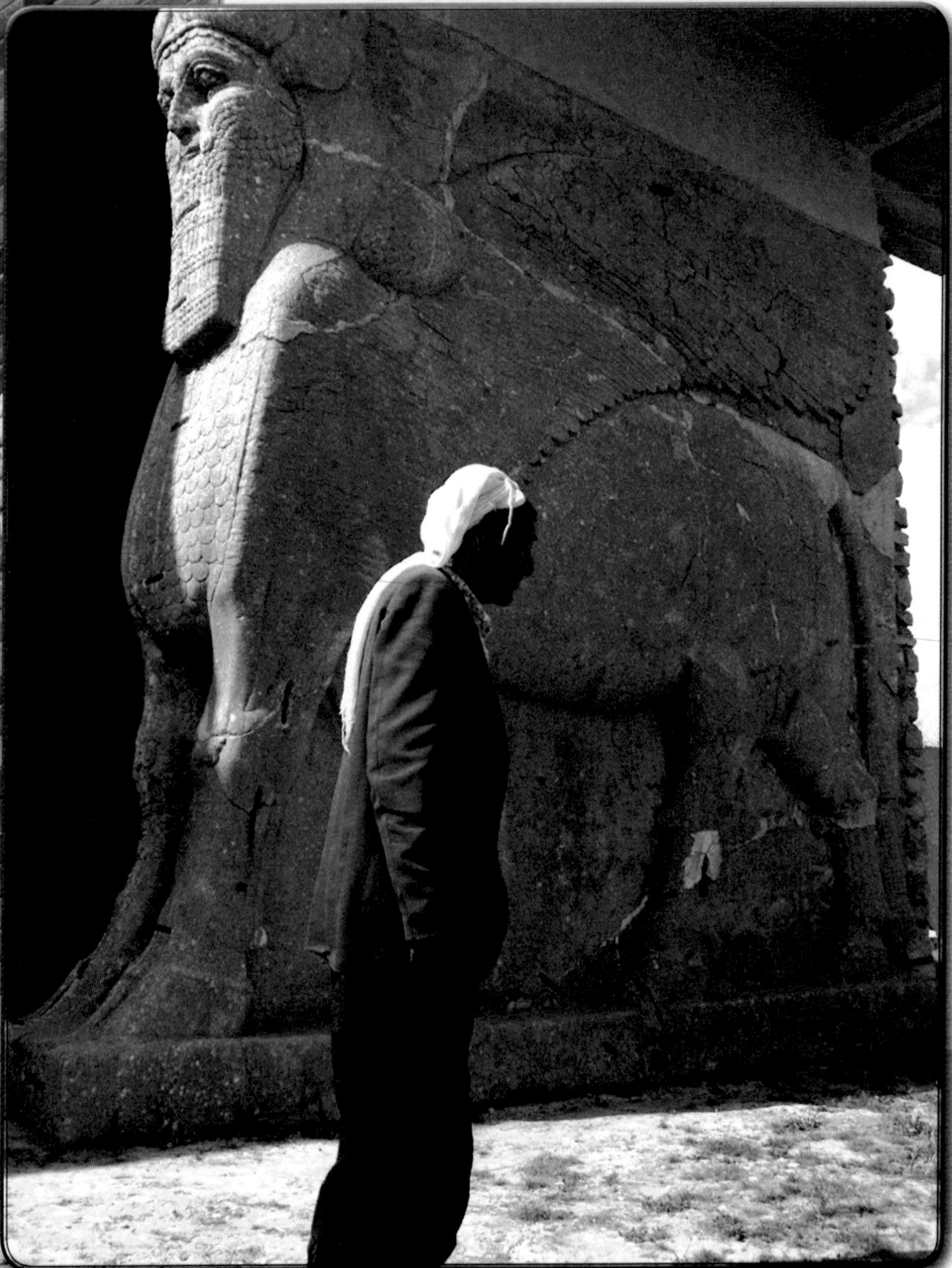

palaces and temples. The Assyrians produced little literature, but in great libraries they preserved copies of Babylonian and Sumerian works. They worshiped the old Babylonian gods but gave their own god, Assur, first place.

After the death of Ashurbanipal, Assyria's enemies joined forces. In 612 BC the Babylonians and Medes completely destroyed Nineveh. Six years later the Assyrian empire collapsed.

THE CHALDEAN EMPIRE

After the fall of Assyria, Babylonia enjoyed 70 years of independence. The Chaldeans, a little-known Semitic people, became the ruling class of the New Babylonian, or Chaldean, Empire. The most famous of their kings was Nebuchadnezzar II (604–561 BC), who rebuilt Babylon. The Chaldeans made great progress in science—particularly astronomy and mathematics—and strongly influenced the Greeks. From the towering ziggurat temples,

An Iraqi worker stands next to an ancient Assyrian statue of a winged bull with a human face, at the archaeological site of Nimrud, in northern Iraq. **Karim Sahib/AFP/Getty Images**

astrologer-priests read the stars. They could even predict eclipses.

The original city of Babylon stood on the right (west) bank of the Euphrates. Nebuchadnezzar extended the city to the left bank as well and built a stone bridge across the river. The city was in the shape of a square, surrounded by a massive towered wall. Palaces and temples were of vast dimensions.

Nebuchadnezzar's own great palace achieved a touch of fairyland from its famous Hanging Gardens, which the Greeks counted as one of the Seven Wonders of the World. The beautiful Gate of Ishtar spanned Procession Street, which led to the Temple of Marduk, chief god of Babylon. Near it stood a great terraced ziggurat, built in seven receding stories with a sloping ramp spiraling around it to the top. This may have been the original Tower of Babel described in the Bible (Genesis 11:1–9), but it was only one of many artificial "holy mountains" in and around Babylon.

Visitors walk through the newly renovated Ishtar Gate in 2008. **AFP/Getty Images**

THE HANGING GARDENS OF BABYLON

The Hanging Gardens of Babylon have long since disappeared. They were said to have been built by King Nebuchadnezzar in the 6th century BC to please and console his favorite wife, Amytis. Great terraces of masonry were built one on top of the other. On these were planted gardens of tropical flowers and trees and avenues of palms. They were irrigated by water pumped from the Euphrates River. Nebuchadnezzar and his queen could sit in the shade and look down upon the beauties of the city. The walls of Babylon were often included with the Hanging Gardens among the wonders of Babylon. Built by Nebuchadnezzar, they were faced with glazed tile and pierced by openings fitted with magnificent brass gates.

A reconstruction of the city of Babylon around 625 BC, with the Tower of Babel in the distance and the Hanging Gardens built by King Nebuchadnezzar in the foreground. Three Lions/Hulton Archive/ Getty Images

LATER HISTORY OF MESOPOTAMIA

Known for his military might, Nebuchadnezzar II ultimately carried his conquests to the border of Egypt, though the days of his empire were numbered. He died about 561 BC and was succeeded by his son Awil-Marduk. In about 600 BC the Indo-European peoples from the northern grasslands, who later conquered and settled all of Europe, started moving into Mesopotamia and taking over this prized territory. The first of these, the Medes, took Assyria and then fell before Cyrus the Great as the Persians spread their empire to the Mediterranean; Babylon itself, capital of the Chaldean Empire, was taken by the Persians without fighting in 539 BC. The Persian Empire lasted more than two centuries, until the conquests of Alexander the Great. Alexander the Great died in Babylon in 323 BC after adding Mesopotamia to his many conquests.

Then Roman legions came, but in AD 363 they gave way before Persia, whose Sassanid kings established their capital at Ctesiphon. Finally the Arab Muslims took control of Mesopotamia in the 7th century AD. They soon developed into a major world power, and their caliphs built dazzling Baghdad for their capital.

The rise and fall of kings and nations meant little to the farmers plowing the fertile soil. Their rich crops paid for palaces and temples and armies. The Mongol invasions

This engraving shows Macedonian king Alexander the Great in a chariot at the head of his army as they triumphantly enter the city of Babylon, 331 BC. **Stock Montage/Archive Photos/Getty Images**

began in the 13th century. Timur Lenk's raid in 1393 almost depopulated Baghdad. As the Mongol armies poured in from the east, they destroyed the precious canals as they laid waste the countryside. The country did not pass completely into the power of the Ottoman Turks until 1638, but Mesopotamia never regained its ancient fertility, wealth, and splendor. The Ottoman rule lasted until the end of World War I, when the new nation of Iraq was formed with King Faysal I on the throne. Since that time, Iraq has experienced a number of upheavals, most recently in the aftermath of the U.S.-led invasion of Iraq starting in 2003, which led to deposing its dictator, Saddam Hussein. The Iraq War caused widespread death and destruction, but a new Iraqi government has been formed, adding another chapter to the region's long and ancient history.

CONCLUSION

S cholars today continue to assess the achievements of ancient Mesopotamian civilization and strive to gain a clearer understanding of how the civilization influenced its neighbors and successors. The complexity and highly varied nature of ancient Mesopotamia have presented problems for researchers, however, as the civilization had numerous languages and cultures, its history is broken up into many periods and eras, and it had no permanent capital city. The variety of ancient Mesopotamia stands out from other civilizations with greater uniformity, particularly that of Egypt.

While other civilizations may be better known, it is difficult to overstate the importance of many of the accomplishments of the ancient Mesopotamians. The Sumerians, especially, made tremendous advances during the centuries they tilled the land between the Tigris and the Euphrates. Among other contributions, they were responsible for the first known system of writing, cuneiform; the development of the city-state; and the invention of the potter's wheel, the sailboat,

and the seed plow. Technical accomplishments were perfected in the building of the ziggurats, with their huge bulk, and in the large and elaborate irrigation systems. Each of the groups that conquered Mesopotamia during the next 2,000 years absorbed and enriched the Sumerian civilization. The First Dynasty of Babylon advanced trade and commerce and gave to the world one of its first great law codes, the Code of Hammurabi. At Nineveh the Assyrian king Ashurbanipal established the first known systematically collected library. Above all, the literature of the ancient Mesopotamians is one of their finest cultural achievements, as the legends, myths, and epics they created came to be echoed and re-echoed in distant lands. Efforts by scholars and archaeologists to shed more light on ancient Mesopotamia should help bring about a fuller appreciation of the achievements and creativity of these remarkable people.

alabaster A compact fine-textured usually white and translucent gypsum often carved into vases and ornaments.

alluvial Composed of loose soil or sediments eroded, deposited, and reshaped by water.

apportion To divide and share out according to a plan.

bureaucratic Describes a government characterized by specialization of functions, adherence to fixed rules, and a hierarchy of authority.

caliph A successor of Muhammad as temporal and spiritual head of Islam; used as a title.

coalition A temporary alliance of distinct parties, persons, or states for joint action.

cuneiform Writing system composed of or written in wedge-shaped characters.

eclipse The total or partial obscuring of one celestial body by another.

ensis Leaders of city-states in ancient Mesopotamia.

epic A long narrative poem in elevated style recounting the deeds of a legendary or historical hero.

ideogram A picture or symbol used in a system of writing to represent a thing or an idea, but not a particular word or phrase for it.

irrigation The watering of land by artificial means to foster plant growth.

manslaughter The unlawful killing of a human being without express or implied malice.

navigable Deep and wide enough to be traveled by boats or ships.

niche A recess in a wall especially for a statue.

odyssey An intellectual or spiritual wandering or quest.

shekel Any of various ancient units of weight; a unit of value based on a shekel weight of gold or silver.

silt Loose sedimentary material, usually deposited by a river.

smelt To melt or fuse (as ore) often with an accompanying chemical change, usually to separate the metal.

stela A carved or inscribed stone slab or pillar used for commemorative purposes.

stylus An instrument used by the ancients for writing on clay or waxed tablets.

tariff A schedule of duties imposed by a government on imported, or in some countries exported, goods.

ziggurat An ancient Mesopotamian temple tower consisting of a lofty pyramidal structure built in successive stages with outside staircases and a shrine at the top.

The Avalon Project
The Code of Hammurabi
Lillian Goldman Law Library
127 Wall Street
New Haven, CT 06511
(203) 432-1608
Web site: http://avalon.law.yale.edu/ancient/
    hammpre.asp
This project, run by Yale University,
    includes a number of translations of
    the Babylonian Code of Hammurabi
    with helpful information about these
    ancient laws.

The British Museum
Department of Ancient Mesopotamia
Great Russell Street
London WC1B 3DG
United Kingdom
Web site: http://www.mesopotamia.co.uk
The British Museum houses an unparal-
    leled collection of artifacts from ancient
    Mesopotamia. They have information on
    the culture, as well as artifacts displaying
    ancient cuneiform.

The Canadian Society for Mesopotamian
    Studies
University of Toronto

4 Bancroft Ave, 4th Floor
Toronto, ON M5S 1C1
Canada
(416) 978 4531
Web site: http://projects.chass.utoronto.ca/
    csms/main.html
The Canadian Society for Mesopotamian
    Studies was founded in 1980 by a group
    of specialists and interested public
    who shared an interest in the archaeol-
    ogy, literature, culture, and history of
    Mesopotamia. Presently they hold lec-
    tures and symposiums for the further
    study of this ancient culture.

Journal of Cuneiform Studies (JCS)
Boston University
656 Beacon Street, 5th Floor
Boston, MA 02215-2010
(617) 353-6570
Web site: http://www.bu.edu/asor/pubs/jcs/
    index.html
Founded in 1947, the *Journal of Cuneiform Studies*
    presents technical and general articles on
    the Mesopotamian writing system of cunei-
    form. The journal is published once a year.

Oriental Institute of the University of Chicago
Collection: Mesopotamia

1155 East 58th Street
Chicago, IL 60637
(773) 702-9514
Web site: http://oi.uchicago.edu/museum/
    highlights/meso.html
The Oriental Institute of the University of
    Chicago has an excellent collection of
    artifacts due to expeditions to Iraq in the
    early 1900s. The material that has been
    brought back from these expeditions
    forms one of the major world collections
    covering in depth the civilizations of
    ancient Mesopotamia.

WEB SITES

Due to the changing nature of Internet links,
Rosen Educational Services has developed an
online list of Web sites related to the subject
of this book. This site is updated regularly.
Please use this link to access the list:

http://www.rosenlinks.com/ancv/meso

BIBLIOGRAPHY

Apte, Sunita. *Mesopotamia* (Children's Press, 2010).

Danti, Michael D., and Zettler, Richard L. *Sumer and Its City-States* (Cobblestone, 2003).

Faiella, Graham. *The Technology of Mesopotamia* (Rosen, 2006).

Fitterer Klingel, Cynthia, and Noyed, Robert B. *Ancient Mesopotamia* (Compass Point Books, 2003).

Gruber, Beth, and Wilkinson, T.J. *Ancient Iraq: Archaeology Unlocks the Secrets of Iraq's Past* (National Geographic, 2007).

Hunter, Erica C.D. *Ancient Mesopotamia* (Chelsea House, 2007).

Landau, Elaine. *The Assyrians* (Millbrook Press, 1997).

Malam, John. *Mesopotamia and the Fertile Crescent, 10,000 to 539 B.C.* (Raintree Steck-Vaughn, 1999).

Mehta-Jones, Shilpa. *Life in Ancient Mesopotamia* (Crabtree, 2005).

Nardo, Don. *Science, Technology, and Warfare in Ancient Mesopotamia* (Lucent Books, 2009).

Oakes, Lorna. *Mesopotamia* (Rosen, 2009).

Reece, Katherine E. *The Mesopotamians: Conquerors of the Middle East* (Rourke, 2005).

Rustad, Martha E.H., and Hiti, Samuel.
    The Babylonians: Life in Ancient Babylon
    (Millbrook Press, 2010).
Schomp, Virginia. *Ancient Mesopotamia:*
    the Sumerians, Babylonians, and Assyrians
    (Franklin Watts, 2004.)

INDEX